Restful

A 30 Day Adventure Learning to Trust
God Completely

But be sure to fear the Lord and serve him faithfully with all your heart; consider what great things he has done for you.

I Samuel 12:24

Restful

A 30 Day Adventure Learning to Trust
God Completely

Meschelle Kolb

Published by: K2 Development Institute

2017

First printing 2017

ISBN 978-0-578-19229-1

Published by K2 Development Institute
P.O. Box 915
Middlebury, IN 46540
www.meschellekolb.com

Ordering Information:
Special discounts are available on quantity purchases by corporations, associations, educators, and others. For details, contact the publisher at the above listed address.

U.S. trade bookstores and wholesalers:
Please contact K2 Development Institute at 574-318-8955 or email at: mk@meschellekolb.com

To Bret

I will love you forever and ever and then some,

and more than that ... just for starters!

TABLE OF CONTENTS

Acknowledgements 9

Forward 10

Relationship - The Foundation of Trust

Day 1   The Need for Relationship 14

Day 2   The Power of Relationship 19

Day 3   The Result of Relationship 22

Day 4   The Act of Relationship 26

Day 5   The Growth of Relationship 30

Day 6   The Hope of Relationship 34

Day 7   The Identity of Relationship 39

Day 8   The Truth of Relationship 44

Day 9   The Choice of Relationship 47

Day 10   The Thrill of Relationship 51

Trials - The Development of Trust

Day 11   Waiting In Trials 57

Day 12   Letting Go In Trials 60

Day 13   Persevere in Trials 63

Day 14   Endure in Trials.. 66

Day 15   Believe In Trials.. 70

Day 16   Hope in Trials.. 73

Day 17   Growth in Trials 76

Day 18   Be Strong in Trials.................................... 79

Day 19   Perspective in Trials................................. 83

Day 20   Realignment in Trials 89

Joy - The Result of Trust

Day 21   Joy Involves Perception............................ 94

Day 22   Joy Involves Release 98

Day 23   Joy Involves Rest..................................... 101

Day 24   Joy Involves Peace................................... 105

Day 25   Joy Involves Hope.................................... 108

Day 26   Joy Involves Beauty 112

Day 27   Joy Involves Consistency 115

Day 28   Joy Involves Patience............................... 119

Day 29   Joy Involves Contentment 122

Day 30   Joy Involves a Promise 125

Acknowledgements

I wish to thank with all my heart those of you who have walked the journey of life with me and shared the stories that I write about. To those of you who have believed in me even when I didn't believe in myself, I owe everything.

First, it was my parents. You have encouraged, supported and loved me for my entire life. Your attic is full of all my stories and creations since I started writing. It now stores copies of every single blog post or article that I write. Your belief in me is an inspiration to follow my dreams!

Next, I found the love of my life, Bret. I know you would give anything for me to be happy and successful. You have seen potential in me when I couldn't and you have sacrificed so that I can pursue my passion! Thank you for loving and believing in me.

To my children: Derek, Brittany and Hunter. You have lived these stories with me and watched me grow in my faith. Thanks for your love and patience. I pray that you will experience a full relationship of trusting in God as you live your own lives!

Foreward

Trust - it seems like a simple concept on the surface. I first remember hearing the word as a Sunday School song: "Trust and obey, for there's no other way to be happy in Jesus than to trust and obey." The dictionary defines trust as a reliance on the strength or ability of another person or thing. Simple. I have learned over the years, though, that simple and easy are two very different things. The concept is simple - not complicated. But the application is hard because it requires us to take our eyes off of ourselves and put them wholly on God.

Although I have been in a relationship with God since I was a little girl, my trust in Him is a work in progress. My life has had some really great times. I have been blessed to be married to the love of my life, Bret, for 26 years, and we have three wonderful children and an amazing daughter-in-law. But, it has been through the hard times that I have really learned how to trust.

In the course of our marriage, we have lived in 13 different locations. That averages out to be a different house every 2 years! The biggest move that we had was going to Alaska. We spent five years in Alaska and God used that time to teach us many things. Being far away from anything that felt "normal" and four time zones away from any other family or friends, I started to experience God in a whole new manner. When life felt out of control and I knew I was powerless to influence it, I started to learn for myself what trust in God really looked like.

In this devotional book, I share stories from the last seven years that God has used to shape my trust in Him. It is a journey of learning how fully trusting God helps us to find rest.

It is my prayer that God will use my stories and this book to help you grow in your relationship with God. I pray that you will learn how to let go, trust God completely and find rest in Him!

Relationship:

The Foundation of Trust

1

Day 1   The Need for Relationship

If we claim to be without sin, we deceive ourselves and the truth is not in us. If we confess our sins, he is faithful and just and will forgive us our sins and purify us from all unrighteousness.

I John 1:8-9

My family and I lived in Alaska for five years. Having spent my entire life in the mid-west or eastern United States, the move was very traumatic for me. I thought that we were moving to the "middle of nowhere." In most ways, life in Alaska was more normal than I expected. The scenery and wildlife, however, were much grander than I anticipated. Moose were a common sighting, much like deer in the mid-west. They inspired me to write this parable.

The Parable of the Moose

Once there was a successful and beautiful Alaskan woman. As she went about her daily life, she encountered many moose. One Sunday afternoon, while driving home with her daughter, she rounded a corner in her neighborhood to find a moose standing right on the edge of the road. Aware of the danger, the excited teenage daughter yelled out the window, "Be a good moose and don't run into the road."

The very next morning, as the woman's family was waking up, the same daughter noticed another moose in their neighbor's yard. The family had an incredibly naughty and naive pet dog who was, at that time, on the chain in the backyard. Aware of the danger that the moose presented, the thoughtful mother at once brought the dog inside to the safety of their home.

This same woman, however, had encountered other moose one month earlier. These particular moose were sleeping in the snow. They were hard to see as they had camouflaged themselves quite well among the bushes and shrubs.

Ignoring the danger because they looked so cute and innocent sleeping in the snow, the foolish woman walked out into the yard and approached them to take pictures.

Oh you foolish Alaskans, you think that a moose has danger just because it looms right in front of you, yet you ignore the danger of the moose in your own backyard. Many of you will crash into moose as they run across the road, but many more of you will be gored and attacked by those that hide in your own backyard.

As Jesus spoke privately to his disciples later, he might explain to them that the moose represent sins and temptations in their lives. He might say that, as we acknowledge the danger of the moose on the side of the road, we also acknowledge the "big" sins in life. Many people are entrapped by those sins, but many more are ruined by "innocent" sins that they ignore on a regular basis. These little habits and innocent sins are just as offensive to God as the big ones.

Sin is not a popular topic these days, I know, but it can't be ignored. Sin is simply anything that we do which is wrong. Just like in the parable of the moose, it is easy to identify the "big" sins: murder, grand larceny, kidnapping and all the things that land people in federal penitentiary. We look at people who commit those sins as "bad," but we tend to ignore the sins that we commit on a daily basis. What about those "little" sins of stretching the truth, justifying a bad attitude, cursing under your breath at the driver who cut you off? Just because you don't go to jail for them and no one else knows about it, doesn't make it right.

READ

Romans 3: 1-31

THINK ABOUT IT

Each of us, no matter how good we are or how important we are, sins on a daily basis. God is holy and just, demanding perfection. That creates a big problem; our sin gets in the way of a relationship with God. The only way to get to Heaven is to be perfect, which we definitely cannot do on our own. Because of our sin, we deserve eternal death and separation from God. This problem was solved by Jesus Christ. Jesus came to earth as God the Son. He died on the cross to pay the penalty for our sins. Since He was the only perfect person, He is the only one qualified to be our sin replacement. If you ask Him to forgive your sin, He will wipe away the penalty for your sin, be your Savior and give you the right to be with Him in Heaven for eternity.

Sin is the reason each of us needs a relationship with Jesus. He loves us and wants that relationship also. If you have never asked Jesus to be your Savior, you should do that right now. Here is a sample prayer, if you don't know how to begin.

"Dear God: Now that I understand who Jesus Christ is and what He did for me, I want to receive you as my Savior. I do believe that you are the Son of God and that you died on the cross to pay the penalty for my sin. Please come into my life, forgive my sin and

make me a member of your family. I now turn from going my own way. I want you to be the center of my life. Thank you for your gift of eternal life and for your Holy Spirit, who has now come to live in me. I ask this in your name. Amen."

If you just prayed that prayer, you are now in a true relationship with Jesus Christ. This is an exciting journey and I am glad to be on it with you!

2

Day 2   *The Power of Relationship*

Keep this Book of the Law always on your lips; meditate on it day and night, so that you may be careful to do everything written in it. Then you will be prosperous and successful.

Joshua 1:8

It was a normal day; my kids, Brittany and Hunter, were running late to school and they rushed out the door in a last-ditch effort to get to class on time. Within a few minutes they crashed back into the kitchen in a mild hysteria. Brittany's car wouldn't start. After I flew in with my superhero cape and saved the day by chauffeuring them to school, I called my husband, Bret, to discuss the problem. We had just purchased a new battery a few months earlier, so we knew that wasn't the issue. Maybe she left her lights on (again), maybe there was an electrical short somewhere, or maybe it was a much bigger issue like the ignition switch. That evening, Bret put on his own "Super Daddy" cape and started to investigate the problem. He was mentally ready to spend hours working on it and he had several possible problems to check out. Within 20 minutes, however, the car was running and he was back inside. It seems that when we replaced the battery a few months earlier, one of the connectors did not get reattached completely. There was a bad connection which was limiting the power from the battery. When Bret got it securely fastened, everything started working again.

The same is true with our personal lives. Our power source needs to be the Word of God and our relationship with Christ. If we become unattached and quit reading our Bible or spending time in prayer, we lose our power. Our relationship with God is what gives us strength, direction, hope and purpose. Luke 11:28 says, "Blessed are those who hear the word of God and obey it." Blessed means to be happy or favored. That doesn't mean that we won't have trials in our lives, but it does mean that God will be working in us and He will bring us peace. God also promises to give us direction and wisdom through His word. Psalm 119:105 says, "Your word is a lamp for my feet, a light on my path."

READ

Jeremiah 10:12-16

THINK ABOUT IT

Sometimes when we are feeling discouraged or downhearted, we look for complicated solutions but the problem is simple and staring us straight in the face. Like my daughter's loose battery connection, maybe we need to get plugged back into the source of true power and find our strength in Christ.

Our relationship with God is strengthened by our daily interactions with Him – Bible reading and prayer. This is how we get our true power and ability to stand against the evil in our everyday life.

Are you plugging into God's power source on a daily basis? If you aren't spending time in prayer, you aren't connected so He can give you power for your day. Why don't you spend the next 10 minutes talking with God? If you choose to focus on Christ, He can energize you with His love!

3

Day 3   The Result of Relationship

*Love the Lord your God with all your heart and with all your soul
and with all your mind.*

Matthew 22:37

Some of the adventures we had in Alaska still make me
smile, like our annual trek to see the Independence Day
fireworks display in Anchorage. Like many things, this is
different in Alaska than in most parts of the country. For
starters, it doesn't get very dark in the summer in Alaska, so
there aren't a lot of fireworks displays. The city of
Anchorage, however, has a nice display and we attended
almost every year we lived there.

It was an hour drive into Anchorage, so we would start
planning a few days in advance, making it a day long trip

going out to dinner and finding other fun things to do. The only complicated part of this planning, however, was that they never announced a starting time. It was set to start "at the conclusion of the baseball game which started at 9:30 pm." Really?

One year, we drove into town and got to our perfect viewing spot around 11:00 pm. Other people had already arrived and set up their chairs, so we hoped that the fireworks would be starting soon. Since it was chilly, sprinkling, and the mosquitoes outnumbered humans 1,000 to 1, we decided to stay in the car as long as possible. As midnight approached, though, we left the comfort of the car and staked out the perfect viewing spot on the grass. We spent another enjoyable half hour swatting mosquitoes waiting for the baseball game to end. I remember having the thought that when the teams are the farm team of the farm team of the farm team of the farm team for the major league, by the time midnight rolls around not even the starting pitcher's wife or mother cares who wins the game. Yes, we were starting to get a little grumpy. Around 12:30 the game finally ended and the fireworks began. As my son, Hunter, pointed out, though, after midnight they become Fifth of July Fireworks – another oddity of living in Alaska!

The fireworks were big and loud, which was good. My family appreciates the loud ones – the ones that make your stomach vibrate. My oldest son, Derek, said that they could just fire off canons and it would be fine with him. The ride home was fun and crazy as we discussed very important topics like why aliens always abduct women with rollers in their hair who live in trailer parks.

The next morning, however, we had to pay the price for our Fifth of July fireworks trip. We got to bed around 2:00 am, and the alarm clock started ringing 4 hours later, at 6:00. When it went off, I asked my husband, Bret, if he intended to get up or if he was going to snooze it for a while. His grunt indicated that he had no intention of getting up for a little while. We tried to ignore the alarm clock for at least 30 minutes and, every 7 minutes as I snoozed the alarm again, I crawled back into bed fully intending to snooze it again the next time. I know it doesn't make sense, but we intentionally set the time early so that we could ignore the alarm for a while.

READ

Matthew 16:24-27

THINK ABOUT IT

Do we ever do that with God? Do we go to church, pray or read our Bible dutifully out of habit, with no intention of fully surrendering to God? Do we engage in these habits just like we set the alarm … because we know we should, but fully intending to ignore it for as long as we can? The result of relationship with God should be love, devotion and commitment, not just habits that mean nothing. Remember, if we don't truly invest in our relationship with God, it will eventually mean nothing. If you aren't already doing so, make sure that your habits of attending church, reading your Bible and praying are more than empty habits. Invest in them with true devotion and love so that you can grow closer to God!

4

Day 4   The Act of Relationship

For God so loved the world that he gave his one and only Son, that whoever believes in him shall not perish but have eternal life.

John 3:16

What is love? That is a question that has been pondered for centuries. Some cultures have the luxury of using several words to define the different forms of love. In English, however, we are stuck using one word to describe some vastly different concepts. How would you describe love - real love?

I know there are Biblical terms which are much more exact, but this is my version. The first aspect of love is happiness. "I love pizza, I love having the family together, I love opening packages at Christmas." Second, there is a sexual aspect of love, which I think needs no explanation at all. If you need clarity, just turn on your television ... enough said. Third, there is a general feeling of charity and well-being toward others. This is the idea of showing respect and courtesy instead of always being selfish. Lastly, though, is what I call real love. Although the other aspects of love involve happiness and can be somewhat self-serving at times, real love isn't always fun. Real love hurts sometimes.

In a strange way, our dog got me thinking about this topic of real love during the last months of his life. Sam lived to be 17 years old. We think he was mostly blind because his pupils were completely clouded over, he could barely hear anything, he had such severe arthritis in his hips that he could no longer get up by himself, he slept at least 90% of the time only waking up and barking in the middle of the night, and he lost control of some of his bodily functions. It got to the point that it was easy to complain about him, wondering why we even had him anymore. He really served no purpose. The answer was love. Real love involves serving others even when they are incapable of giving you anything in return.

Real love doesn't just appear, it takes time to grow. When I think of Sam I know that my love for him grew slowly over the last 17 years. My husband surprised me with Sam when our daughter was just three weeks old. I did not want him and would have given him away to any willing person for at least the first year of his life. But gradually he became a part of our family to the point that I truly loved that crazy dog.

For his last several months, I took care of him even though he couldn't do anything in return.

Our society tends to overlook that part of love. We all want it from others, but so many people aren't willing to give it. We have become selfish and started defining love as what someone else can give to us. But that focus is wrong. Real love involves what we can give to others not what they give in return.

READ

Matthew 26-28

THINK ABOUT IT

Jesus came to earth completely for our benefit. He gave up Heaven and confined himself to an earthly body which was a complete sacrifice on his part. He got nothing so we could get everything. That is real love. His entire earthly adventure was a sacrifice with the ultimate culmination of suffering on a cross for us. That is love - painful, raw and real.

Our relationship with Christ should result in that act of love also – love for Christ and love for others. Does your love for Christ change the way that you act on a daily basis? Are you truly committed to Him or is it just a matter of convenience?

Also, are you investing in anyone else to the point where it hurts? Are you willing to sacrifice for the benefit of anyone else or are you expecting others to make you happy? It is when we start taking our eyes off ourselves and putting them on the needs of others that we start showing real love.

5

Day 5   *The Growth of Relationship*

For I am convinced that neither death nor life, neither angels nor demons, neither the present nor the future, nor any powers, neither height nor depth, nor anything else in all creation, will be able to separate us from the love of God that is in Christ Jesus our Lord.

Romans 8:38-39

My husband, Bret, and I have been married for 26 years! It is hard to believe that it has been that long or that we are that old!

When we were first married, I thought that the most romantic people were the young, newly married couples. The ones who, like us, were starry-eyed and full of fairy tale dreams of happily ever after. I looked at older couples, like my grandparents, who were wrinkled and holding hands walking down the street. I appreciated that they were still in love, but I felt sorry that they didn't have the dynamic relationship that we had. I sure didn't have a clue ...

With 26 years of experience now, I am just starting to understand what true love and devotion are all about. Yes, we were in love when we got married, but our love has grown into so much more through the experiences (both fun and challenging) that we have shared together. We started out young, broke and clueless living in married student housing at Cedarville College. Since then, we have lived in 10 different cities, Bret has changed jobs several times, we have bought and sold 6 houses, changed countless diapers, mediated hundreds of sibling fights, experienced sickness, disappointment, crushed dreams, and the joy of creating new dreams. We had no way of knowing the path that our life together would take; the only thing we knew was that we were walking that path together. In our wedding, Bret sang the song, I Will Be Here, by Steven Curtis Chapman. Through the song, he promised that, regardless of the circumstances of life, he would be there for me through it all – and he has. I have joked with him on occasion that I wished he would have put a location in that song so that I could know from year to year what city I would be living in. But the point is, no matter what city we live in or what circumstances we are experiencing, he will be there for me and I will be there for him. That is the essence of true love. It isn't the starry eyes or the romantic candle lit dinners, though those are nice. It is the commitment that we will choose to love each other even after we truly know each other. When life is tough and we realize that "happily ever after" is a lie, we know that we still have each other.

A few years back, Bret and I were in a small group Bible study on marriage. In it, our pastor emphasized that the true purpose of marriage is to model our relationship with Christ. Ephesians 5 talks about the roles of a husband and wife in marriage, and it concludes in verse 32 by saying "This is a profound mystery—but I am talking about Christ and the church."

READ

Ephesians 5:21-33

THINK ABOUT IT

If God gave us marriage as a picture of His relationship to us, as the church, then there is a lot to learn about God through our marriages. Just like my relationship with Bret has grown deeper through the years, so does my relationship with Jesus Christ. I realize that it has been in the hard times where Bret and I have grown closer, and so it is with Christ. As we walk through the trials of life, it is an opportunity to experience the love of God even more.

In the same way that so many people bail on their marriages when things get tough, many people bail on God in times of trouble also. People tend to think that both spouses and God are there to make them feel happy; when they are no longer happy they look other places for their happiness. But real relationship is so much more than happiness. Real relationship grows through the years in both the happy and the sad times.

God wants you to know Him in a real way. He has not promised to take away our trials, but He has promised to be with us in everything. As our relationship grows, we start to experience what real love really is.

Let me encourage you that if you are in a time of trouble, don't bail on your relationship with God. Lean into His love. If you do this, you can look back in the years to come and see how He showed His love to you even in the midst of it all. Your relationship will grow through the trials!

6

Day 6   The Hope of Relationship

Trust in the Lord with all your heart and lean not on your own understanding, in all your ways submit to him, and he will make your paths straight.

Proverbs 3:5-6

My husband, Bret, and I like to do minor house remodeling projects. Here is the time frame for most of our projects:

1. Complain about the current situation for a couple months.
2. Decide impetuously that we can accomplish the entire project in one weekend.
3. Establish an unrealistically small budget.
4. Go to Lowe's that morning and purchase less than the needed supplies.

5. Start project that same day with high hopes.
6. By the end of the weekend, and after 4 more trips to Lowe's, we are about half way done.
7. After two weeks, the project is complete. It looks wonderful and we never bother to add up the multiple receipts which, if we did, would be way over budget.

When we purchased our house in Alaska, it had a 3 foot by 12 foot deck that was strictly a walkway to the stairs to go down to the back yard. Besides being too small to use, it was old and not very sturdy. Unlike our approach to completing most home projects, we planned the deck project for over a year. We went to Lowe's one Friday morning with a detailed shopping list and optimistic dreams. We had several other appointments scheduled for Friday, so the goal of day one was shopping and destruction of the old deck.

We got up Saturday morning excited about the project. Everyone was motivated and excited to see progress. Unfortunately, things were slow at the beginning as it involved intense measuring and leveling. The ground in that part of Alaska was 95% rocks. Maybe that was a slight exaggeration, but not much. Every time we would dig out another rock it would throw the level completely off. Eventually, we got the support posts installed (even level) and then the fun began. It wasn't easy work, and it may have included 6 additional trips to Lowe's, but we did get it finished in one weekend!

Aside from the sheer joy of having a deck that was big enough to use and built solid so that you didn't fear that it would collapse, we had a huge sense of accomplishment that we actually got it done in one weekend.

As we talked about it afterward, we realized that we shouldn't let past performance determine our present action. Just because we had attempted projects in the past with poor planning and unrealistic goals, that didn't predict our success with the deck project.

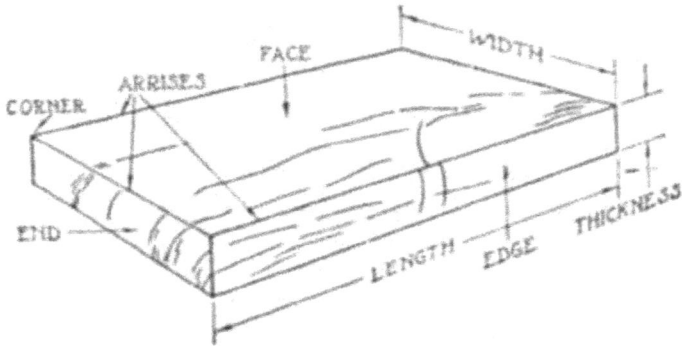

READ

John 6:16-21

THINK ABOUT IT

Spiritually speaking, we need to understand that, even though we have miserably failed God in the past, that doesn't mean that He can't use us now or again in the future. Here is where the analogy to the deck breaks down a bit. With the deck, it required better planning, realistic goals, and good time management on our part. In our relationship with Christ, there is nothing we can do on our own.

A few years back, I heard a sermon from John 6 that applies to this idea. In John 6:16-21, Jesus is walking on the water toward the disciples who are in a boat. The waters were rough, the wind was blowing, and when the disciples saw a figure coming toward them, they were understandably afraid. In verse 20, Jesus says to them, "It is I; do not be afraid." The pastor explained that when Jesus says "do not be afraid," it is originally in the Greek passive imperative verb tense. He said that this is used for a command that is impossible for the people to do. Strictly speaking, Jesus was telling the disciples to do something that He knew they could not accomplish on their own. A better translation would be "You give me your fear, right now." If they would choose to give Jesus their fear, He could take care of it. There was no way, however, that they could do it on their own.

There have been many times in my spiritual journey with Jesus that I have tried to obey him and do great things for Him out of my own strength – and failed each and every time. It is hard for me to understand that I have no ability to serve Him on my own. It is only by completely giving my life and myself over to Him that He can fully use me for His purposes. But, just like our deck project, things can be different this time. It is a daily decision to completely surrender to Him and let Him work in me – not try to accomplish anything on my own.

That is the hope of our relationship with Christ. We give Him our fear and failure and He produces the results!

7

Day 7   *The Identity of Relationship*

A good name is more desirable than great riches; to be esteemed is better than silver or gold.

Proverbs 22:1

When we lived in Alaska, I was amazed by how many coffee huts there were. I'm not talking about the standard Starbucks, but little huts on almost every corner that sell all different varieties of coffee. I know that fancy coffee is popular almost everywhere, but in Alaska, probably because it tends to be colder, coffee is almost a religion.

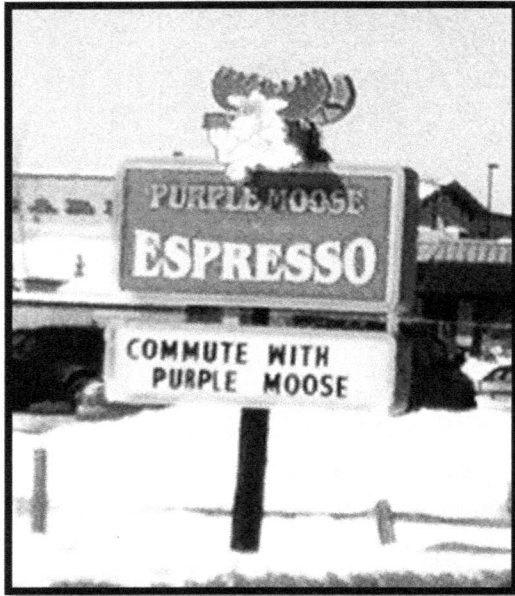

There was a coffee hut near my house called The Purple Moose. One day, I saw this sign and it got me thinking. Moose aren't supposed to be purple; so if I drink your coffee I will start seeing purple moose and they will commute into Anchorage with me. Yikes ... I think I will avoid the coffee laced with hallucinogens. Another coffee hut is named "Mocha Me Crazy." Let me get this straight, if I drink your coffee I will start having psychotic episodes ... no thanks, my life is crazy enough without your coffee.

I know, I know, I was carrying this a little too far. They are just cute, catchy names that are designed to get your attention. I am all for cute, but when did we start coming up with names that are meaningless? There is absolutely nothing about "The Purple Moose" or "Mocha Me Crazy" that tells me how wonderful their coffee is or why I should go there instead of Starbucks.

Some names do have meaning, though. For example, when we lived in Alaska we had a new boiler installed. (For those of you not familiar with boilers, they are heating systems quite popular in Alaska.) We had the boiler installed by Hardy Heating.

We knew the owner; Dan Hardy was Hunter's football coach. He and his son spent an entire day at our house installing the new boiler. Then, less than an hour after he got home and after 9:00 at night, he came back to our house because we found that something wasn't working quite right. The next morning he called me to make sure there weren't any problems. A few days later, he came back again to add some extra supports to ensure that the unit was stable. Now, I am quite sure that Dan's level of customer service and quality of work are just a part of his character and he would perform at an equally high level even if his company was named "Hallucinating about Purple Moose Heating Specialists." I think that having his name on the company ups the ante a little bit, though. His name and his character are tied to his business so he wants to make sure that his work holds the highest standard possible.

READ

Acts 11

THINK ABOUT IT

I don't think that names mean a lot to us these days. Sometimes children are named after relatives or influential people in their parents' lives, but for the most part I think that parents pick names because they are cute or popular. It wasn't always this way. In the Bible, names held special meaning. God even changed some people's names to indicate a special event or promise. God changed Sarai's name to Sarah to symbolize his covenant with her and with Abraham; Jesus changed Simon's name to Peter to symbolize his new kingdom; and Saul's name was changed to Paul when he trusted Christ after his experience on the road to Damascus.

We take the name and title of Christian, but do we really appreciate what it means? The term Christian originally meant "little Christ." As we live our lives as Christians, Christ's name, character and love are intimately entwined with us. Non-believers see Christ in us even on our bad days. We should be proud of our name, but we need to wear that name carefully so that we bring glory and honor to Christ and not shame. Maybe we need to think about that on a daily basis so that, as we run errands, drink coffee with purple moose, or merely interact with people at work or the grocery store, we proudly show Christ's love to everyone we interact with.

8

Day 8   *The Truth of Relationship*

*And we know that in all things God works for the good of those
who love him, who have been called according to his purpose.*

Romans 8:28

I'm not one of those people who spends hours playing
games on my phone or computer. Frankly, I don't have time
for that. But, occasionally, if I get to school early I will play
spider solitaire on my phone while waiting for the kids. I
have other more popular games loaded on my phone, but
they were downloaded by my kids. I only play them when
the kids feel they need to challenge me in order to justify
their desire to play. Usually, after they annihilate me once
or twice in a head-to-head challenge, they bore with me and
play by themselves. I find two suit spider solitaire fun,

though. It is challenging enough to make me think and strategize, but also able to be beaten. (Especially because I choose to deal winning hands instead of random deals.)

One day when I actually got to school early, I played a game of spider solitaire. I wasn't doing very well, and I got to the point of dealing out the last cards from the stock without having completed any sequence runs. (If you are not familiar with spider solitaire then just know that it was nearing the end of the game and I had not accomplished any of the objectives.) As the last cards were dealt out, though, I had the exact cards in the perfect places so that I was able to complete all the runs and win the game. Prior to that last deal, I didn't anticipate winning the game. I couldn't see any way to complete the sequences. Even if I had taken the time to plan exactly which cards I needed and where they needed to be placed, it would have been too complicated for my little brain to figure out ahead of time. But after the cards were dealt, I could see one move at a time and each move created another move which worked together to accomplish the goal.

READ

Psalm 24

THINK ABOUT IT

In a strange way, I think that my life is like a game of spider solitaire. Because I'm a Christian, I know that I have a winning deal. God has told me in the Bible how it will all end, so I am confident that life will work out eventually. Even when the board of my life doesn't make sense and the cards seem random and out of order, God know exactly which cards I need to make the runs fit together perfectly (though maybe not how I expected or planned).

Every time that I play spider solitaire and experience an unexpected win, I am encouraged about God's work in my life. I have intentionally set out on a path to see God in every area of my life so I look for ways to apply God's truth. His promises are true and consistent and, if we search, we can see them evidenced in all areas of our lives.

How about you? Are you seeking after God in every area of your life or are you content to be a Sunday Christian? God is present in every situation and trying to teach us things every single day. Often, though, we don't acknowledge Him as we are too busy running our lives by our own agendas. Why don't you try intentionally seeking after Jesus and let Him speak to you – it's an amazing journey!

9

Day 9   The Choice of Relationship

*Choose for yourselves this day whom you will serve, whether the
gods your ancestors served beyond the Euphrates, or the gods of
the Amorites, in whose land you are living. But as for me and my
household, we will serve the Lord.*

Joshua 24:15

I have never claimed to have a green thumb. Most of my
plants die shortly after I bring them into my home. In fact,
my children used to apologize to plants that I would buy,
knowing what their fate would inevitably be!

I have had a Christmas Cactus for the last year and a half.
Even though it had never bloomed, I counted it a success
that it was even still alive. When I was decorating for
Christmas last year, I ran out of room on my kitchen counter

so I placed a small table in front of the window and moved all my plants there. Despite the fact that I moved the plants for my benefit, not theirs, the change was amazing. After moving them in front of the window, they started getting regular sunlight and they all started blooming. The Christmas cactus had 28 blossoms that year! One little change made a huge difference.

Our relationship with Christ is, in a way, similar to the story of my plants. We may know that things are growing stagnant; we don't feel close to God. Sometimes this manifests itself in feelings of depression, anxiety or fear. Sometimes it ends up with serious sin issues. Even though we may realize that something needs to change (like how I took care of my plants), it is often easier to keep things as they are. In order to change our relationship with God (or anything for that matter) we need to make a choice to change. If we want to have a real relationship with Christ, we need to choose that and then act accordingly.

READ

Hebrews 11

THINK ABOUT IT

All the heroes of the Old Testament mentioned in Hebrews 11 were commended for their faith and their choice to follow

God. Abraham chose to follow God's command and move his family, even though he didn't know where he was going. He later chose to take his son, Isaac, up to offer him as a sacrifice even though it didn't make any sense. Noah chose to build an ark even though it seemed outrageously crazy to everyone else. They had faith and they made the hard choices to follow God's command because they were in relationship with Him.

I think that each of the people mentioned in Hebrews 11 made one major choice – to be in a real relationship with God. After that, the other choices or outward actions that got mentioned in the Bible were easier. One they said "yes" to a relationship with Christ, the other choices just seemed natural.

They weren't perfect. Each of them also had examples of making the wrong choices. Abraham, for example, lied about his relationship with his wife, Sarah, for his own protection. He also had a relationship with Hagar when it looked like it was too late for Sarah to have children. Because of his primary decision to be in relationship with God, however, he is remembered for his victories, not his failures.

Each of us also has the choice whether or not we will be in a growing relationship with Christ. That is the major decision which, like moving my plants, can have a lot of positive implications. We, like Abraham, will also have our failures, but we can still choose to ask forgiveness. God will restore us and we can continue to grow in our relationship with Him.

You have the option to be in a growing relationship with the God of the universe – but it is your choice. What will you choose today?

10

Day 10　　The Thrill of Relationship

So do not fear, for I am with you; do not be dismayed, for I am your God. I will strengthen you and help you; I will uphold you with my righteous right hand.

Isaiah 41:10

When you live in Alaska, you have two options: huddle up inside all winter (which lasts almost 7 months some years) or figure out how to have fun in the snowy, cold weather. During our time there, one of Derek and Hunter's answers to wintertime boredom was snowboarding. After one storm that produced 14 inches of snow in one day, we got an unexpected snow day. Unexpected because Alaskans pride themselves in being tough, so most don't let a minor thing like slippery roads stop them from doing anything – even going to school.

On this rare snow day, we decided to go snowboarding in one of the local mountains. The area is called Hatcher Pass and it has a 2 mile skiing/snowboarding trail. You drive to the top to drop off the snowboarders and then pick them up again at the bottom, eliminating the worst part of snowboarding or sledding – the walk back to the top. Brittany decided not to go sledding or snowboarding – she and I had a bad experience earlier that year. We both panicked (though at different times) resulting in us running into multiple trees, rolling down a significant part of the trail and coming to the end with our hair completely encased in ice because we had been in the snow so much. Because of this, she decided to take pictures and keep me company as I was the designated driver.

It is fun to remember that trip and all the fun the boys were having. Derek never had a lesson, but he could snowboard really well. Somehow, he just had a knack for it. Hunter was still learning to snowboard and he definitely had more than his share of falls, but he kept going back and trying the snowboard again. What made them so eager to go snowboarding when Brittany and I were more than content to stay in the truck and drive them around?

It could be the y chromosome (I blame a lot on y chromosomes) or it could be the bad accident that I had sledding 10 years ago when I hit a log and broke my tailbone, or it could be my first experience snowboarding which was more appropriately termed as "falling down a hill with my feet strapped to a board." I don't know exactly what the reason is, but I really don't appreciate the sport anymore. There is something about feeling out of control sliding down ice that really scares me.

I think that you need to be able to let go and enjoy the thrill of the ride, not concerning yourself with the trees, jumps, or possibility of a concussion. That is something that I cannot seem to do anymore. I have become too safe and too concerned about permanent bodily injury.

READ

John 15

THINK ABOUT IT

Isn't it that way with our Christian life? In order to really experience God, we need to let go and stop concerning ourselves with the perceived threats or dangers. We need to trust Him completely and enjoy the ride of life. Sure, He may take us out of our comfort zone, and we will definitely hit a few trees and jumps along the way (but, honestly, hitting the trees and jumps happens anyway even when we try to be in control). But isn't the ride worth it? He not only makes the ride of life enjoyable, but He makes it count for eternity also. So, maybe it's time to get on the snowboard of life and trust God to take us where He wants us to be – letting go of control and letting Him totally lead the way!

Trials:

The Development of Trust

11

Day 11   Waiting In Trials

Be still before the Lord and wait patiently for him; do not fret when people succeed in their ways, when they carry out their wicked schemes.

Psalm 37:7

When we bought our home in Alaska, we knew that the front porch wasn't going to last too long. The wood was showing signs of rotting, so we planned to remove it altogether, replace it with a flower bed and install a nice walkway.

Phase 1 of the project, which involved removing the rotting porch and putting in the flower bed, went very quickly and easily. Phase 2 was the installation of the walkway. It became more involved that we initially hoped it would.

We actually researched this project and found out that we would need to dig at least a foot down to create a solid base and keep the stones from shifting. It seemed like the dirt was comprised of 20% dirt and 80% rocks, so after an entire weekend of digging, we were not even half way done. For a couple weeks, it looked like we had a shallow grave in our front yard. It was a hard process digging out the rocks, moving the dirt and ensuring the ground was level when we finished. We spent several weeks working on the foundation of the walkway to ensure that the stones would stay level and solid when it was complete. Instead of rushing to complete our project in a weekend, like we usually do, we actually took our time to make sure that the project was done right.

READ

Lamentations 3

THINK ABOUT IT

Waiting during trials is hard. We want to get through them as quickly as possible and get on with the fun part of life. Trials, however, are the foundation for a strong relationship with Christ. God uses them to grow our character and teach us things that we wouldn't learn during the easy times. That process, much to our dismay, takes time and waiting.

Although we wanted to lay the stones for our walkway that first weekend, we needed to wait for the digging to get done and the foundation of gravel to be laid and leveled. If we had put in the stones any earlier, it would have been a complete waste of time.

In the same way, we may want certain things to happen in our lives or the lives of our loved ones, but there are steps that God is doing right now that need to be accomplished first. By trusting Him, actively pursuing Him, and waiting on His timing, then we will see His glory revealed. We all need to be willing to wait on the Lord during trials.

12

Day 12   Letting Go In Trials

Have I not commanded you? Be strong and courageous. Do not be afraid; do not be discouraged, for the Lord your God will be with you wherever you go.

Joshua 1:9

When we moved to Alaska, one of my biggest fears was getting attacked by a bear. The leadership of the camp we worked for probably thought twice about letting our family join their ministry after my interrogation of their evacuation plan when a person gets mauled by a bear. Notice, I did not say "If a person gets mauled by a bear," but "when a person gets mauled by a bear." I used to think that I would be out in the flower bed happily pulling weeds when a vicious bear would stroll around the corner and rip me to shreds. (As if I am ever happily pulling weeds …)

After three years in Alaska, I had not seen even one bear. Derek and Bret had both seen bears in Anchorage of all places. Derek saw a black bear on the army base each summer that he was at JROTC camp. Bret got his first sighting when a bear ran across the Glenn Highway during rush hour! That summer, he often saw a bear sitting on the side of the road as he would drive to or from work. Since he saw this bear so many times, he gave him a name – "Buttercup."

After three years without a sighting, I eagerly wanted to see a bear. I'm wasn't crazy and wishing that one would show up in the backyard, but I wanted to see one on the side of the road posing for a nice picture. I never did see Buttercup that summer. In fact, it wasn't until we were planning to move out of state that I finally saw a bear. Funny enough, he was sitting on the side of the interstate in Anchorage and we stopped to take pictures.

READ

I Peter 5:6-11

THINK ABOUT IT

I think we all have irrational fears that, if we were being honest, drive what we do, what we think and how we react to situations. How much of your day is spent worrying? How does that amount compare to the amount of time spent praying, sharing Christ with others, or even dreaming about the possibilities of the future? Experts say that 85% of what people worry about never even happens. Because we are wasting so much time thinking about the horrors that may happen, we have less time to do what Jesus really wants us doing.

Don't you think that if we truly believed that God's will was the best for us that we would be able to relax and accept what He sends our way instead of worrying about what our worst fears are? I know that it is much easier said than done, but if we really had faith then I think that it would show itself in joy and peace, regardless of the circumstances. If I really want to listen to Jesus and do what He wishes, then it is much less about what I want and much more about the opportunities that He brings my way. I am striving to listen to Jesus more and to then humbly do what He tells me to do, without question or fear. Would you accept that challenge also? Instead of telling Jesus what He needs to do, let's be quiet and listen to Him more.

13

Day 13   Persevere in Trials

Blessed is the one who perseveres under trial because, having stood the test, that person will receive the crown of life that the Lord has promised to those who love him.

James 1:12

Last summer, I decided to tackle another home project. I had some old patio furniture that I thought was un-salvageable. It was worn out, weather-beaten and even rotted in spots. No one ever sat on the bench because it looked like it would fill you with splinters if you got too close. I did use the wheel barrow as a planter, but the rotted spots made you think twice before putting in too many plants. At the beginning of the summer I debated if it was worth fixing them up or if they should just be trashed.

My daughter, Brittany, offered to paint them for me as long as she got to pick the colors. After some scrubbing, sanding and a few coats of paint, they looked like completely different. They both started out gray and weathered. Now, the bench is bright blue with a big yellow sunshine on the seat. The planter is bright yellow with red flowers overflowing the sides. Once dingy and ignored, they are now some of the focal points of our backyard.

READ

Philippians 4:6-8

THINK ABOUT IT

Many times, our lives can be like these old pieces of furniture. We see the problems, frustrations and ruts that we are living in. We then start debating if it is worth the effort to fix the problem and climb out of the rut - maybe it would be easier to just start over.

Let me urge you today not to give up. Climbing out of a rut takes work just like we had to spend many hours cleaning and painting our furniture out in the hot sun. If you put in the effort, though, it can make a tremendous difference.

Here are four simple steps to start seeing real change today:

1. Admit the reality of where you are. If you are stuck in a rut, there is probably a lot of emotion tied to your current situation. Try to take the emotion out of it and factually evaluate your issues. What are the good points and the bad in your life right now?

2. Pray about these issues. God loves you and He knows everything going on in your life. Please note that this is not a sure-fire way to get what you want. Sometimes God lets us stay in hard situations to build our character. Ask God for guidance as you complete the next two steps.

3. Pick one area to start working on. It is unrealistic to try to address every issue at once. Resist the urge to tackle everything and just pick one to start with.

4. Do one thing today to address the issue. It may be a huge situation that may take a while to completely solve, but you can start seeing progress if you take one action step today!

14

Day 14   *Endure in Trials*

Endure hardship as discipline; God is treating you as his children. No discipline seems pleasant at the time, but painful. Later on, however, it produces a harvest of righteousness and peace for those who have been trained by it.

Hebrews 12:7,11

It was four o'clock in the morning and my husband and son were standing in the Pacific Ocean, arms locked with 9 other guys to ensure that the surf didn't wash them out to sea. After 12 hours of physical training the day before and a mere 3 hours of sleep, they were abruptly awakened at two o'clock in the morning with blow horns sounding in their dorm. They had already run two miles to the beach, conducted battle simulations and endured an hour of physical training. Now, struggling against the waves, a battle-tested instructor was yelling at them to stand strong and "embrace the suck."

Mark Divine, a former Navy Seal and director of SealFit, the program Bret and Derek were attending, describes the concept of "embracing the suck" this way. "Embracing the suck is developed by leaning hard into challenges" in order to become stronger (*Unbeatable Mind,* page 157). Another soldier defined it this way, "Face it, soldier. I've been there. War ain't easy. Now deal with the difficulty and let's get on with the mission" (*Learning to 'embrace the suck' in Iraq,* Los Angeles Times, January 28, 2007).

Members of the military know that their jobs aren't always easy or fun, but they are committed to the mission so they do them anyway. If they quit when things get tough, their life, the lives of their fellow soldiers and the ultimate mission will be in jeopardy. "Embracing the suck" is the only way to survive and make it home in one piece. I think that this mindset applies to our spiritual and emotional lives as well.

READ

Ephesians 6:10-12

THINK ABOUT IT

Jesus says that, as Christians, we are in our own battle against sin and the Devil. The Message version of the Bible translates these verses as "God is strong, and he wants you strong... This is no afternoon athletic contest that we'll walk away from and forget about in a couple of hours. This is for keeps, a life-or-death fight to the finish against the Devil and all his angels" (Eph. 6:10-12, The Message). But, a lot of the time we forget that. We think that life is about our happiness and comfort. When trials come, we whine, complain and beg God to take it all away instead of acknowledging that it's just part of life and God actually uses these trials to help us grow.

Let's face it, sometimes life sucks. Chances are good that you are facing some trials right now. How are you looking at those challenges? Are you holding your own personal pity party that life isn't fair, begging God to take away the pain, or even ignoring the problems in order to live in a false sense of peace? Today, as we each face the hardships of life, let's commit to "embrace the suck," lean into our trials and let God use them to help us grow stronger.

15

Day 15   Believe In Trials

Why, my soul, are you downcast? Why so disturbed within me?
Put your hope in God, for I will yet praise him, my Savior and my
God.

Psalm 42:5

Recently, I was running late. My family would read that
sentence and say, "So, what else is new?" But on this day it
mattered to me to be on time. I had been at an appointment
almost 3 hours from home and I needed to pick up my kids
from school. It was important that I got there on time
because I had to take Brittany directly to work after
school. Stopping to get lunch, I knew that I had exactly 15
minutes to eat before I had to be on the road. I went to my
favorite place - Panera Bread. Excitedly I walked into the

store and took my place in the long line of people. After patiently waiting my turn, I quickly placed my order. As luck would have it, the iced coffee that I ordered was empty; so, I nicely informed one of the employees. But brewing the coffee takes time and, of course, he got delayed because the iced tea machine started brewing all over the counter and floor. I won't bore you with all the other delays that I endured during my "quick" lunch stop, but they resulted in me leaving 15 minutes later than I had originally planned.

I am quite proud to say that I wasn't upset or frustrated when I left. My dad would say this is a fault of mine - that I don't care enough about punctuality. But, on this rare occasion, I really did care; I just didn't let myself get worked up. Recently, I have been trying to internalize the message from the quote by Charles Swindoll.

"We cannot change the inevitable. The only thing we can do is play on the one string we have, and that is our attitude...I am convinced that life is 10% what happens to me and 90% how I react to it. And so it is with you...we are in charge of our attitudes."

As I left the restaurant and started my trip home, I knew that I would be cutting it close to get there on time. I focused on maintaining a positive attitude, though, so that I didn't ruin the entire drive. Interestingly enough, a short time later traffic slowed and eventually stopped due to a traffic accident. As I watched the police cars arrive, it became apparent that the wreck had recently happened. I realized that if I had left on time, I may have been involved in that accident. I have no way of knowing, of course, but it is possible that God allowed that coffee carafe to be empty, the tea to spill over and all the other events that seemed "bad" at the time in order to prevent me from being in that wreck. As I passed the scene of the accident, I prayed for those involved and thanked God for delaying me from leaving on time.

READ

Romans 5:2-5

THINK ABOUT IT

If we believe that God is in control of everything, then how can we class events as "bad?" Maybe we need to stop assigning value judgments to life events and start living intentionally, with good attitudes, no matter what comes our way. It may just change our lives!

16

Day 16   Hope in Trials

His pleasure is not in the strength of the horse, nor his delight in the legs of the warrior; the Lord delights in those who fear him, who put their hope in his unfailing love.

Psalm 147:10-11

The clouds, fog and gloominess were threatening to consume Northern Indiana. It was just a typical January, but it was starting to feel intense. I had only seen the sunshine for one glorious day that week. Other than that one day of respite, we were living in the middle of a giant cloud. The weather was affecting attitudes and productivity, not to mention hairdos!

We lived in Alaska for 5 years and experienced our share of dark, gloomy days in January. This may be hard to believe, but the darkness in Alaska wasn't as hard to deal with and I finally figured out why. The darkness in Alaska can be tracked with the sun. It is predictable year after year and everyone knows when it will end. After the winter solstice, everyone starts tracking the increase in sunlight each day. It's in the newspapers and reported each night on the news stations. I knew people who lost the sunlight completely at their homes for a period of time because of their proximity to a mountain. They could tell me exactly what day the sun would come over the mountain again and cast its warm rays on their house. They looked forward to that day all winter. Most Alaskans chose to focus on the increasing sunlight instead of the darkness.

It's different in Indiana. We don't know when the sun will return because it's definitely not being blocked by a mountain. It's not based on certain patterns; it's just random cloudy days so it's easy to get lost in it and forget that the sun will indeed return again. The same can be true in our lives.

READ

I Peter 1:6-9

THINK ABOUT IT

We all go through periods of trial and difficulty. It may be an illness, a relationship problem, stress at work or a myriad of other trials. And our trials don't come with a published termination date. With no foreseeable end in sight, it can be easy to get lost in that trial and forget that it will eventually end and peace will come again.

So, what's the secret? It's all about perspective, what we choose to focus on. Are you going to focus on your problem? If so, you can expect to be consumed with fear, anxiety and exhaustion. Or, you can choose to focus on something else - God's love in the midst of the trial, what you are learning through the trial or something outside of the trial completely. What you focus on will drive your attitude, energy and hopefulness.

If your life feels dark and gloomy, you can be assured that the proverbial sun will shine again, even if you don't know when. If you choose to focus on God's love and all His promises you just may see sunshine in the midst of the storm.

17

Day 17   Growth in Trials

Make every effort to add to your faith goodness; and to goodness,
knowledge; and to knowledge, self-control; and to self-control,
perseverance; and to perseverance, godliness; and to godliness,
mutual affection; and to mutual affection, love.

II Peter 1:5-7

Blueberry picking was one of our favorite fall activities in
Alaska. I remember one of the first trips we made out into
the mountains to pick blueberries. It was the beginning of
the blueberry harvest so we had to really hunt for them. We
got a few buckets full of blueberries, but the most
memorable part was when Derek got bored and started
squashing blueberries into Hunter's head. His blond hair

was distinctly blue for the rest of the day. Thankfully, it didn't stain and by that evening he looked normal again.

Another time, we took my parents who were visiting from Indiana. We spent an entire day driving through the mountains and, even though we heard of several bear sightings in the area, we picked 6 buckets of blueberries and 2 buckets of fireweed blossoms. The next day, while the kids were in school, Bret, Mom, Dad and I crowded into our little kitchen to make countless batches of blueberry jam and fireweed jelly. That, in and of itself, was an adventure I will never forget. My dad usually only enters the kitchen to eat, so he turned it into quite a fun adventure, giving more than a little commentary about the amount of sugar used to make jam.

Did you know that, although all blueberries are very healthy for you, blueberries grown in Alaska have the highest amounts of antioxidants and are, by far, the best blueberries in the world? Apparently the more stress that a plant has to endure, the more antioxidants it will produce. The harsh Alaskan climate produces the best berries.

READ

James 1: 1-8

THINK ABOUT IT

I think that our lives are like blueberry plants. The trials that we face give us the opportunity to trust God more and to become stronger. Although it isn't natural to see difficult situations as blessings, they are truly the times where we grow the most and develop into useful vessels for Christ. If we want to be strong and solid Christians, then we must endure stress and trials.

It isn't easy for me to see problems as blessings, so I have tried to change my approach to prayer lately. Instead of asking God to remove a problem, I have been striving to ask Him to show me how He can use it for His glory. All of life (the good and the bad) can be used for God's purposes. Let's use times of stress to become more like the Alaskan blueberry – strong and hearty in our faith, not wimpy and useless.

18

Day 18   Be Strong in Trials

*But he said to me, "My grace is sufficient for you, for my power is
made perfect in weakness." Therefore I will boast all the more
gladly about my weaknesses, so that Christ's power may rest on
me. That is why, for Christ's sake, I delight in weaknesses, in
insults, in hardships, in persecutions, in difficulties. For when I
am weak, then I am strong.*

II Corinthians 12:9-10

Home improvement projects have such good application
principles. Our home in Alaska needed a lot of work, so we
spent most summer weekends fixing it up. In fact, the kids
said that the theme for summers in Alaska was "Hi Ho, Hi
Ho It's Off to Work We Go." I remember one weekend
when the plan was to finish off the walkway in the front

yard. Unfortunately, not all the supplies were delivered in time. We would have had all of them, but I made a minor miscalculation on the amount of sand needed. I overlooked the detail of cubic yards versus cubic feet, and it turned out that we needed 27 times more sand that I thought ...oops!

For this reason, our weekend project was changed to level and re-seed the backyard. This involved moving two entire dump trucks full of dirt from the front yard to the back yard. Bret, Hunter and Derek got the job of shoveling the dirt into the ATV trailer, Bret then drove it to the back yard where I dumped, spread and leveled it. It took the entire weekend and a lot of sweat and hard work, but the finished product was amazing. It only took a few weeks of long summer days for the grass to come in nice and thick. Before too long, we forgot how bad it was initially.

Although I talk a lot about home improvement projects, I am not by nature a rugged and wild woman. I would choose cute fashion over Carhartts any day, the biggest animal that I have ever killed is probably a spider, and 9 times out of 10 I would choose shopping over hiking. But that being said, I am not a wimp. I am very willing to pull my weight and do my fair share of the work. Over the years, I have been on the roof to fix gutters and shovel snow, I have helped replace a sewer line (on our anniversary, no less!), I have cleaned wild game and fish, and I have hauled and stacked wood since I was little.

READ

Luke 22

THINK ABOUT IT

The disciples had a similar story to mine. On the outside, they were just normal men that, prior to meeting Jesus, had worked as fishermen, tax collectors, and in other ordinary professions. Nothing about them seemed powerful or influential, except for their time with Jesus. In essence, on their own they were genuine wimps. Peter even denied Jesus three times prior to Jesus being crucified. On their own, they were just men. Men who wanted significance but had no way to find it. Men who wanted to make a difference but didn't have a platform. Men who didn't have the strength to stand for what they knew was right.

Their time with Jesus and the Holy Spirit within them, however, made all the difference in the world. Peter became a powerful apostle and was used by Jesus to start the early church. He, along with the other disciples, changed from cowardly men hiding in an upper room afraid of the Roman soldiers into powerful witnesses for Jesus. That change was the Holy Spirit. Once they were no longer controlling their own lives and they gave control to the Spirit, they became spiritual heroes.

On our own, we are also spiritual wimps. We cannot do anything of significance without the Spirit. Letting go of control and trusting Jesus to lead you can be scary at times – but, through Him, we will see amazing things happen!

19

Day 19   Perspective in Trials

Being strengthened with all power according to his glorious might so that you may have great endurance and patience, and giving joyful thanks to the Father, who has qualified you to share in the inheritance of his holy people in the kingdom of light.

Colossians 1:11-12

Football is very important to my family. Every fall, regardless of what state we live in, we fly The Ohio State Buckeye flag. Our passion for cheering for the Buckeyes is second only to cheering for our own sons on the football field. Derek and Hunter played for many years, both starting in 2nd grade. One of the most memorable football seasons, however, was when Derek was in 11th grade and Hunter was in 7th.

Derek had his best football season that year. When the season began, he was the starting wide receiver for the JV team. In the first game of the season, he made several catches and averaged more than 10 yards after the catch. He almost caught a 2 point conversion but another player on his team ran the wrong route and jumped in front of him for the catch. And then … he caught a pass in mid-field, outran all the defenders and scored his first high school touchdown! He had such an outstanding performance during that game that he was called up to Varsity. By the end of the season, he was one of the starters.

(I had to include this picture because, even though Derek and Hunter have both scored multiple touchdowns in their careers, this is the only touchdown picture that I have. Usually I am too involved screaming to even think about the camera. Yes, I am one of those mothers.)

Unfortunately, Hunter's season was not as stellar as Derek's. He had a tough time because he was a 7th grader on a 7th / 8th grade team. How this played out was that all the 8th graders and the couple guys who had already hit their growth spurt in 7th grade played most of the game. There was a rule in community "non-competitive" football that all the players would play at least 5 downs during a half. So, the little guys comprised the secondary offense and they played their mandatory 5 plays and then got taken off the field. Hunter was a running back, with an offensive line that averaged 80 pounds. They played against teams that usually didn't substitute all their little guys at once, so the defensive line usually averaged around 135 pounds. It wasn't a pretty sight. Hunter would get a hand-off, shockingly, the line would collapse and he would get flattened under 10 defensive players.

As I watched Hunter that season, I was really proud of him. He only played 10 plays each game, he probably never made positive yardage, and he got beat up pretty badly …

but he didn't give up. As he came off the field one time half limping and trying hard to hold back tears, one of the other moms looked at me quizzically and asked if I was going to go and see if he was fine. I'm not trying to sound crass and uncaring, but because this was football and it is pretty much a given that you will feel some pain during the game, I let him work through it on his own. We did talk afterward and I remember telling him how very proud I was of him.

READ

Psalm 27

THINK ABOUT IT

Sometimes the hard times are good for us. Sometimes God brings trials into our lives knowing that we will get hit pretty hard by the opposing lineman, but knowing that is exactly what we need to toughen us up. We all have issues in our lives that mirror Hunter's football experience. The coach told him to run up the middle and he knew that a kamikaze pilot in World War II had a better chance of survival than he did, but he did it anyway. He got bruised and hurt during the process, but he emerged at the end of the season as a tougher man.

When we have difficult circumstances, do we ask God to take us out the of game until the line is smaller, or do we follow His orders, run ahead and see what he will teach us along the way? I was inspired by my son and I hope that you can be inspired to keep going in your Christian life also!

20

Day 20   Realignment in Trials

Many are the plans in a person's heart,
but it is the Lord's purpose that prevails.
Proverbs 19:21

Have you ever started something with a fool-proof plan and all the necessary ingredients for success, but things didn't end up quite as you planned? What can you do when you find yourself in a "jam?"

Recently, I had a great idea to turn some old grapes into grape jam. I found a quick and easy recipe, what could go wrong? I was excited as I stood at the stove stirring my jam; it smelled delicious and I started imagining my family feasting on warm biscuits with home-made jam for dinner. The recipe said that it would require 25-30 minutes of boiling for the jam to thicken. Although it seemed to start to thicken around 15 minutes, I don't claim to be Martha Stewart, so I followed the instructions and boiled it for the required time. It seems that I forgot one important detail; I was only using a small amount of grapes (1/4 of the recipe) so there was less liquid to boil off. I boiled off enough liquid that when my jam completely cooled, it was a giant grape rock!

Thankfully, I have lived long enough to laugh at my kitchen mishaps. Oh well, the grapes would have been thrown out anyway. I was sure it was worthless, but I kept my rock so that everyone else could get a good laugh. Hunter, though, saw other possibilities. He broke off a piece and told me I had cracked the secret code for making jolly ranchers. So, instead of grape jam we had grape candy!

READ

Jeremiah 29:10-14

THINK ABOUT IT

Isn't this true of our lives also? We come up with a plan, but when things don't work out like we want them to, we decide the whole venture was worthless. What if we looked at life from another angle to see something good out of the apparent "failure"?

Sometimes, we think that we get to decide the plans, but only God knows the plans for us. We need to trust Him and follow here He is leading, even if it's not where we initially wanted to go.

Trust God today to take you where He wants you to go, even if you don't know where you are going!

Joy:

The Result of Trust

21

Day 21   Joy Involves Perception

Let the heavens rejoice, let the earth be glad;
let the sea resound, and all that is in it.
Let the fields be jubilant, and everything in them;
let all the trees of the forest sing for joy.

Psalm 96:11-12

A few summers ago, life felt out of control. We had been living quite happily in Alaska, with no plans of leaving, when my husband lost his job. Although he applied to several jobs there, the offer that came was across the continent in Indiana. Within one whirlwind month, our oldest son graduated from high school, we sold our house, drove across the continent, moved into a new house, watched our son leave for Army Basic and started making a new life in Indiana.

The next month brought a sense of emptiness to our family - Bret and I had our own issues to deal with as we settled into a new place and tried to adjust to life without Derek, but Brittany and Hunter were completely lost.

One morning, while mowing the lawn, Brittany saw something float down on the top of the lawnmower. She took a closer look and was shocked to see that it was a hummingbird. This little hummingbird just sat on the lawn mower and didn't even try to leave. We were concerned that he was injured, so Brittany gently picked him up. He had no visible injuries, but he made no effort to leave either. He was named "Pip" and was soon Brittany's first friend in the area.

Pip was eager to drink hummingbird food. We thought he would fly away as soon as he regained some energy. But, he had no intention of leaving anytime soon. We finally made him a home out of a shoe box to protect him from anything that might try to eat him overnight. Brittany was sad to tell Pip "good-night" because we were convinced that he would not be alive in the morning.

Amazingly, Pip was squeaking very loudly the next morning. He was happy to see Brittany and get more food. This went on for 3 days and we were starting to

wonder if we had acquired a new pet. He would hop around his box, but showed no interest in flying at all. Then, one day when he was inside due to a major thunderstorm, he decided to start flying - very dangerous in a house with 2 dogs and a cat. We moved him back outside by a flower and within minutes he flew away. We put out a feeder and he came back regularly to eat. On a couple of occasions, Brittany even saw him flying toward her from a tree to say "hi." The next year, he came back and even brought his wife. We have named her "Peep."

I searched online and apparently it is very rare for anyone to get to hold a hummingbird, let alone have one live with them for a few days. As Brittany and I talked about the experience afterward, we decided that God had given her a special gift as a gentle reminder that He loves her and is always with her. The Bible says that we can see God in nature.

READ

Psalm 19:1-4

THINK ABOUT IT

Most of the time we are too busy to notice God around us. I believe that God allowed Pip to come visit Brittany so that we would see Him. God was always there, but we were choosing to focus on everything else. Pip broke the routine and made us take notice of God's creation ... and if God is big enough to create a miracle like hummingbirds, He is definitely able to take care of us when life seems out of control also. Even if you never experience a miracle of nature like Pip, God is still with you - and He is still in control.

22

Day 22   Joy Involves Release

Sing to the Lord, all the earth;
proclaim his salvation day after day.
Declare his glory among the nations,
his marvelous deeds among all peoples.

For great is the Lord and most worthy of praise;
he is to be feared above all gods.

1 Chronicles 16:23-25

My eyes flitted around the room as I tentatively started to raise my hands. The conservative denomination in which I was raised frowned upon public displays of worship, so I had never lifted my hands. As my hands slowly reached higher, though, I felt a freedom and release that I have never experienced previously. That night, for the first time, I raised my hands, sang completely to the Lord and worshiped Him from my inmost soul.

We live in a society that judges us. Especially as women, we feel the need to look a certain way in order to feel accepted by others. We want to be approved and liked for who we are. On the surface, there is nothing wrong with being accepted and fitting in, but we need to be careful that our self-esteem isn't based on that. As I mentioned earlier, I was raised in a very conservative tradition. As a competitive perfectionist, I excelled at following the rules. I never wanted to do anything that would attract negative attention or receive judgement, so I have always been very careful not to stand out in any way. Now, though, those inner limitations can prevent me from "letting go" and fully experiencing an event. It was a breakthrough for me when I fully worshiped that night. I let go of my reservations and sang for God without caring what anyone else thought - and I am sure those around me could hear how off-key I was singing. I am not advocating being rebellious, but if you feel that God is leading you to do something then you should put your entire soul into it, regardless of what others may think.

READ

Esther 4

THINK ABOUT IT

Esther was a very ordinary girl in a horrible situation; yet, God had appointed and anointed her to do an amazing thing for Him and His people. We have also been appointed and anointed by God. You are special to God and He has chosen unique things for you to do. But this is where the urgency comes in. Esther 4:14 (NIV) says, "For if you remain silent at this time, relief and deliverance for the Jews will arise from another place, but you and your father's family will perish. And who knows but that you have come to your royal position for such a time as this?" If we choose not to follow God's leading for any reason - maybe we are too scared, too busy or too insecure to step up and chase the dream He has planted in our soul - then He will find someone else to do it. God's works will not be limited by us, but we can limit our blessing and our involvement. Friend, if God has given you a mission, don't be afraid to follow Him and do it!

When stressful times come for you, let me suggest that you pray, trust God with the results, and then relax! It changes your entire experience! We are all basically the same. We are all, to some extent, scared and insecure about life, but we are on the same mission. We are trying to serve God and do the work He has given us. You have your own mission and unique calling from God. Release your inner constraints and release yourself to fully worship and serve God!

23

Day 23   *Joy Involves Rest*

Come to me, all you who are weary and burdened, and I will give you rest. Take my yoke upon you and learn from me, for I am gentle and humble in heart, and you will find rest for your souls. For my yoke is easy and my burden is light.

Matthew 11:28-30

Groundhog Day has always amused me. To my knowledge, it is the only day where otherwise normal, intelligent people will watch anxiously to see a groundhog predict the weather. I don't really understand the point to it.

Fun fact - according to the official Punxsutawney Phil website, he is correct 100% of the time, which makes him much more accurate than human weather forecasters. I also found it interesting that there has only been

JOY – THE RESULT OF TRUST

one Punxsutawney Phil; apparently he is over 131 years old. According to his website, here's the secret: "Punxsutawney Phil gets his longevity from drinking the "elixir of life," a secret recipe. Phil takes one sip every summer at the Groundhog Picnic and it magically gives him seven more years of life."

To me, the Groundhog Day lore is backwards - if he sees his shadow it means the sun is out which logically tells me that spring is on its way. Nope, it's the other way around; if the groundhog sees his shadow it means that winter is sticking around. It comes from early German settlers in Pennsylvania who had a tradition that if the sun shone on Candlemas Day (the day Jesus was presented at the Temple, celebrated on Feb. 2) the snow would swirl in May. There were a lot of groundhogs in the area, so they became the official mascot to report the sunshine.

READ

Matthew 6:25-34

THINK ABOUT IT

The groundhog story, though slightly ridiculous, is fun and I would say that most of us don't really take it seriously - sorry Phil. Yet we tune in to watch it so that we have some glimpse of what the future looks like, albeit imaginary. Don't we crave to know the future, to feel like we have some advance warning or even control over what happens to us? As people, I think we all instinctively try to control, it gives us some feeling of power in otherwise powerless circumstances. But, if we claim to follow Christ, is that the right thing? Does that fit with the idea of faith?

Michele Cushatt has said, "It's one thing to talk about faith in a God who comes to our rescue, another to live as if you're banking on it. Like it or not, we humans rely an awful lot on our ability to control and manage circumstances. Even worry is an effort to control. But real faith is letting go. A releasing of the what-ifs when everything in you wants to tighten your grip. It's allowing yourself to free fall into the unknown because you have absolute confidence that waiting at the other end are arms big enough to catch you, help you, and make you whole."

Real life and real trust is tough. Trusting God means not trying to take over the driver's seat of life. Have you ever felt that God got something wrong? If we were honest, I think we could all admit to times where we wish we had been running the world. We would have prevented some disaster or decision or illness. We would have come to someone's rescue instead of letting tragedy strike. If you have ever questioned God (and who hasn't) you aren't really trusting Him. Trust is letting go. Period.

We don't know the future and we don't really have control of the present, and that's ok. We have a God that we can trust. We don't understand everything that He does or allows to happen, but we do know that He is love and He loves us.

When we really do let go and trust, it brings rest. If there is something that you are desperately holding onto, maybe it's time to let go. I'm not saying it's easy, but trusting God will bring peace. May you find your rest in Christ today!

24

Day 24   Joy Involves Peace

The Lord gives strength to his people;
the Lord blesses his people with peace.

Pslam 29:11

I recently read this on the internet and it made me smile for the rest of the day.

"I tried the Japanese method of decluttering where you hold every object that you own and if it does not bring you joy, you throw it away. So far, I have thrown out all of the vegetables, my bra, the electric bill, the scale, a mirror and my treadmill."

Joy ... what does it take to have joy? Is it possible to have a life devoid of anything that doesn't bring joy? As referenced above, I don't think that's possible. Throw away the electric bill too many times and you won't have lights.

The Bible even confirms this in John 16:33:

"In this world you will have trouble. But take heart! I have overcome the world."

READ

Psalm 23

THINK ABOUT IT

Yes, this world does have trouble. But Jesus is more powerful than any trouble that the world can bring. He can bring peace in the midst of the war. Psalm 23:5 says,

"You prepare a table before me in the presence of my enemies."

Even in the middle of the battle, with the bullets of life flying right past our heads, Jesus says to sit down and enjoy a nice dinner with Him. A lot of the time, we are so busy watching the bullets and bombs that we don't notice His table - but it's always there for us.

Joy, happiness, peace - it is all a choice. Not always an easy choice but it is always there for us.

If you are in the middle of battle today, I urge you to take a moment and sit down at the feast that Jesus is providing.

Take your focus off the enemy and look into the eyes of Jesus. He loves you and wants you to experience the rest, joy and peace that He is providing.

25

Day 25   Joy Involves Hope

Praise be to the God and Father of our Lord Jesus Christ! In his great mercy he has given us new birth into a living hope through the resurrection of Jesus Christ from the dead, and into an inheritance that can never perish, spoil or fade. This inheritance is kept in heaven for you.

I Peter 1:3-4

When we lived in Alaska, I remember longing for spring. The bleak, colorless days of winter seemed to go on forever! When, in most of the United States, tulips and daffodils had already died back and homeowners were beginning to grumble about their grass growing so quickly, spring was just starting to arrive in Alaska.

The second spring in our house in Alaska, I had an amazing discovery of tulips growing in our flower beds. Tulips are my favorite spring flower, but I had been unsuccessful in growing any since we moved to Alaska. We transplanted over a hundred bulbs from New York and then planted an additional 50 tulip bulbs during our first fall in the house. Not a single bulb grew in our first summer, though, and I decided that bulbs must not grow at all in Alaska. I defiantly declared that I would no longer plant any bulbs. I even went so far as to say that it would be better to only plant silk flowers because they would probably not die. Imagine my shock and joy when I saw 8 tulips growing next to the basement window. My hope was renewed and I tracked them daily that spring. Even though they didn't care, I gave daily tulip updates to my family. Eventually, we had over 30 in bloom at one time!

It's kind of sad how quickly I can get discouraged and how little it takes to derail my enthusiasm.

Designing my first website, for instance, pushed me over the edge more than one time. It took longer than I care to admit to design it and get it fully functioning on the internet. After several weeks, I was ecstatic to finally "go live" with it until I realized that it would not open on smartphones. After two entire days of checking and re-checking all the settings and programming, I was beyond frustrated and willing to give up on the website completely. I have to give credit to my wonderfully patient and supportive husband, though, who encouraged me to keep trying. He came across a suggestion online that, in my limited programming knowledge, made no sense whatsoever. He advised that it was a better idea than throwing the computer out the window (my preferred approach) and eventually that was the fix to the entire problem. So, I am left to wonder … how could I go from ecstasy to utter frustration in two short days?

I think that the answer is found in the eagle. Bald eagles were a common sight in Alaska. I had seen several in zoos in the Lower 48 and knew that they were majestic, but it wasn't until I saw one soaring overhead that I realized how truly awesome they are. Eagles can soar because they use thermals effectively; they float on the wind currents and do not have to flap their wings very much. This saves their energy and allows them to travel faster and further than on their own strength.

READ

Isaiah 40

THINK ABOUT IT

I am in the process of learning that waiting on the Lord is like soaring on the thermals. When I let Him direct my path (floating on the wind currents) he will easily lead me where I need to go. When I insist on flapping my own wings, I get tired very quickly and I really don't go very far. When things go wrong (when I can't grow a single flower, when the website won't work properly), I have two choices. I can either grow increasingly more frustrated and start flapping my wings harder and harder and try to fix the problem on my own; or, I can rest in the fact that God is in control and float on His thermals of peace. The harder I flap my wings the more tired and frustrated I get, but in the times when I choose to let go and trust in God completely, He brings the renewal and peace that He has promised.

The times when life doesn't go as planned are the times when we find out where our faith really is. I know that I need to stop flapping my wings and trust in God and His planning more. How about you? How is God teaching you to trust Him lately?

26

Day 26   Joy Involves Beauty

*In the same way, let your light shine before others, that they may
see your good deeds and glorify your Father in heaven.*

Matthew 5:16

Realtors have told us that initial curb appeal can add several
thousand dollars to the value of a house. In my humble
opinion, we added more than that to the value of our home
in Alaska with our walkway project.

Our house was over 30 years old and the original porch was
still in place when we bought it. Unfortunately, though, it
had seen better days. We knew when we bought the house
that the wood in the porch was starting to rot, but we
weren't expecting to break a hole in it on the first day when
we moved our furniture in. Because we weren't ready to

take on such a big project, we used a large pot of flowers to cover the hole for the first summer. I think I should get points for creativity with that one!

We started the project the next summer with demolition of the old porch, but new construction got put on hold as other things like replacing the septic system and heater took priority. The next summer was construction time and every member of our family put in a lot of hard work to create the finished project. We were quite pleased with how it turned out. It really improved our home's curb appeal.

READ

John 13:31-35

THINK ABOUT IT

How is your curb appeal to non-Christians? I know some Christians who are course and offensive to non-believers, but I wonder how much good they actually do for the Kingdom of God. One of the themes of Paul's writings is that we are to be witnesses through our lives, not just our words. Do you let Jesus live through you so that your actions and emotions show joy, peace and the other fruits of the spirit? Does your life have curb appeal for Christ?

27

Day 27 Joy Involves Consistency

Therefore, my dear brothers and sisters, stand firm. Let nothing
move you. Always give yourselves fully to the work of the
Lord, because you know that your labor in the Lord is not in vain.

I Corinthians 15:58

When we lived in Alaska, one of our favorite winter
activities was riding snow machines, "snowmobiles" to
those of you in the Lower 48. I am really surprised how
much I enjoyed driving a snow machine. I have ridden on
motorcycles my entire life: my dad always had one when I
was growing up and Bret had one for several years. Riding
on the back of a motorcycle has always been boring for me,
except for the short time when my dad convinced my mom
that she needed to drive a motorcycle. I was the smallest so I

had to ride on the back of her motorcycle – that was quite an experience. I did a lot of praying riding on the back of mom's motorcycle.

For that reason, I anticipated that riding snow machines would be rather boring also. The big difference, however, was that I was driving my own snow machine and not riding on the back, staring at someone else's coat. For the first time in my life, I understood the quote from the movie, "Top Gun" – I had the need for speed! My snow machine had a decent sized engine, and I got it up to 70 mph on the lake. Let me be clear, though, that I was not as much of a dare-devil as I would like to think. My line of "too scary to proceed any further" was the same line that told Derek that riding was just starting to become fun.

I remember one winter ride that Derek, Hunter and I took on the lake in our neighborhood. We had one large issue affecting our ability to ride snow machines that season – not all of our snow machines were running properly. Brittany's lost a bolt the season before and, although Bret replaced it, there were some other things that needed to be tuned and adjusted to make it run correctly. In addition, we had sold Hunter's snow machine a few months earlier to upgrade to a larger one. The new one, however, needed a new engine. Bret and Hunter worked for two straight weekends to replace it, but then the carburetor needed to be tuned. This required someone with more experience to finish the job. That being said, that winter we had 5 snow machines but could only ride 3 of them.

So, the boys and I took out Derek's, Bret's and my machine for our ride on the lake. We had a little over an hour of daylight left, so we knew that we had to stay close to home. We rode over our lake and were playing on the adjoining lake when Bret's snow machine decided to stop running. I'm not sure why it stopped, but that wasn't really the issue. The issue became the fact that his pull start would only engage about 5% of the time. I happened to be riding it when it stopped, so there I sat. The boys were doing crazy stunts in the deeper powder (remember, it only becomes "fun" after mom thinks it is too dangerous) so they didn't know about my dilemma immediately. Thankfully, they started to miss me after about 10 minutes and came looking for me. We did have an "Alaskan" method of opening the hood and pulling it by hand, but we were hesitant to try. Eventually, Derek got brave enough to pull it by hand and we were off riding again.

READ

Philippians 1:27

THINK ABOUT IT

As I think about that experience, I realize that, even though we had 5 snow machines, it really didn't carry out the intended purpose because they weren't all reliable and consistent. Bret's snow machine ran great – if it decided to start. But you couldn't count on it starting! Five percent isn't really what I would call consistent.

This doesn't just apply to recreational vehicles. Consistency is a key to our character and our Christian testimony. I am challenged to make sure that my spiritual engine is tuned daily so that I act consistent of God's character on a regular basis.

28

Day 28   Joy Involves Patience

So then, just as you received Christ Jesus as Lord, continue to live your lives in him, rooted and built up in him, strengthened in the faith as you were taught, and overflowing with thankfulness.

Colossians 2:6-7

Living in Alaska involved a lot of home improvement projects. One summer, we had the joy of getting our septic system replaced. It was done in late summer, so there wasn't time for new grass to grow before the snow started. That being said, when the snow melted the next spring, we had a virtual dirt and rock quarry in our backyard. Alaskan dirt is at least 90% rock, so we spent several hours that spring raking the rocks out of the backyard. Then we got 20 cubic yards of topsoil delivered. It took several more hours to get that spread evenly before planting our grass seed. It was back-breaking work, but it was a necessary step if we actually intended for grass to grow.

READ

Matthew 13 and Mark 4

THINK ABOUT IT

Matthew 13 and Mark 4 tell the parable of the sower. Jesus tells the story of a farmer who throws seed on 4 different types of ground: path, rocks, thorny soil, and good soil. Jesus then tells the disciples: "Some people are like seed along the path, where the word is sown. As soon as they hear it, Satan comes and takes away the word that was sown in them. Others, like seed sown on rocky places, hear the word and at once receive it with joy. But since they have no root, they last only a short time. When trouble or persecution comes because of the word, they quickly fall away. Still others, like seed sown among thorns, hear the word; but the worries of this life, the deceitfulness of wealth and the desires for other things come in and choke the word, making it unfruitful. Others, like seed sown on good soil, hear the word, accept it, and produce a crop— some thirty, some sixty, some a hundred times what was sown." (Mark 4:15-20)

Good soil is vital for a good crop. Some soil is naturally good, but other soil needs to be worked with in order to be usable. An investment of time and energy is required before this soil can be usable for the seed. I think that this applies to our spiritual lives also. Sometimes, it takes considerable time and work for God to make us usable soil for Him. We don't like to have a time delay – we want to see immediate results in our own lives and in the lives of others we are vested in (our children, friends, those we are mentoring). But as long as we are truly seeking after God and following His will for us, we need to trust Him for the time it takes to prepare the soil. We need to patient and not quit when our back starts hurting, but keep working until the job is done and the soil is ready for the planting. It is only then that He can truly produce the crop that He is desiring.

Let's keep praying, working and investing in our own lives and the lives of others so that we can be a part of God's plan to produce a bountiful harvest for His glory!

29

Day 29   Joy Involves Contentment

He who began a good work in you will carry it on to completion until the day of Christ Jesus.

Philippians 1:6

Do you have scars? Scars can be any physical or emotional marks left after wounds heal. We often think they are ugly and a constant reminder of hard times so we try to cover them up and pretend they don't exist. But, is there another way to look at our scars and actually think they are beautiful?

I was recently watching a home restoration show on television. The couple bought an old store and turned it into their home. As they toured the camera crew around, they pointed out all the original details that were kept in the final design. These items included the store sign, marble tiles and other beautiful, historical artifacts that did not surprise me. But a few things caught my attention. The couple kept the stair handrails that had gouges and even a gunshot in it. They also kept the original wood entry way that was scuffed and incredibly marked up. They said that those distressed pieces told the story of the building and if they were all replaced, the building would lose its character. Most of the scuff marks were probably just normal every-day wear and tear of a hundred year old store, but the gun shot was obviously an extraordinary event. Although I don't know what happened, I'm guessing it was a low point in the history of the store. At least one person's life was probably altered on that day and the store may have even closed for a while. But, good or bad, it is part of the story of the building.

So it is with our lives. All of us have scars - some we can see and some we can't. By definition, scars are a result of wounds healing. And this always involves pain. For this reason, we often try to hide the scars and try to forget the pain. But, like it or not, those scars represent stories that have shaped us into who we are today.

READ

Philippians 4:10-13

THINK ABOUT IT

We may wish that we didn't have scars, we may wish that we never had to endure the hard times that created the scars in the first place. But God uses them to build our character and shape us into who He wants us to be. We think that our scars make us ugly and unshapely, but God uses them to make us beautiful. They are the stories that have the potential to make us strong - if we choose to embrace them.

Sometimes, we choose to play the victim. Life has been hard; we have scars. So we hide away so no one can see us. What if someone stares or says something rude? We can be embarrassed so we sit around and feel sorry for ourselves. That is a choice that we have, but is it a good choice?

Yes, your scars (both visible and invisible) make you unique and different from everyone else. But if you choose to acknowledge them and grow because of them, then they become just another part of your story. You can use these scars to reach out and help others. Yes, people may still stare or ask questions - but what a great opportunity to tell them about the journey God has brought you through and how He can help them also! Your scars make you beautiful - God loves you and will use you for His glory if you let Him!

30

Day 30   Joy Involves a Promise

No longer will there be any curse. The throne of God and of the Lamb will be in the city, and his servants will serve him. They will see his face, and his name will be on their foreheads. There will be no more night. They will not need the light of a lamp or the light of the sun, for the Lord God will give them light. And they will reign for ever and ever.

Revelation 22:3-5

Alaskan summers are filled with sunshine. Technically speaking on the summer solstice there are 22 hours of daylight. Practically, though, it is bright for all 24 hours. Even though we lived in Alaska for 5 years, it was still a little shocking to walk outside late at night with it bright outside. The lack of darkness even changed our perspective on time.

I remember one night we completely lost track of how late it was getting. Bret and I had been researching some things online and the kids were all hanging out in their rooms when Hunter came and asked me if he could call a friend. My initial reaction was that it would be fine, as we had already planned to invite this friend over the next day. Thankfully, though, I looked up at the clock before he picked up the phone because it was after 10:00 pm. At that point, we determined that the phone call should wait until morning.

We then took the dogs out and walked them without any flashlights and, other than the swarms of mosquitoes, had quite a lovely time, even though it was the middle of the night. As I was outside that night, I remember thinking it was sort of what Heaven will be like. It will never get dark.

READ

Revelation 21

THINK ABOUT IT

These are some glorious descriptions of Heaven that include a city made of gold with the foundations decorated with every sort of precious gem including jasper, sapphire, emerald, ruby, topaz, turquoise, and amethyst. The gates are made of pearl, and the streets are made of gold. It says in verse 23, that "The city does not need the sun or the moon to shine on it, for the glory of God gives it light, and the Lamb is its lamp."

It is easy to get stuck in the hum-drum of life and forget that one day, for those of us who have trusted Christ as our Savior, Heaven is coming. During the long, dark days of winter in Alaska, we had the hope of summer and the endless light to motivate us. As Christians, sometimes life is truly hard and we get stuck in the dark days. We need to remember that Jesus Christ is preparing a wonderful place for us to be with Him forever and that should help motivate us to keep going. As the old hymn says, "It will be worth it all when we see Jesus."

That is truly why we can trust Christ. That is truly our hope and the reason for our joy!

Meschelle Kolb

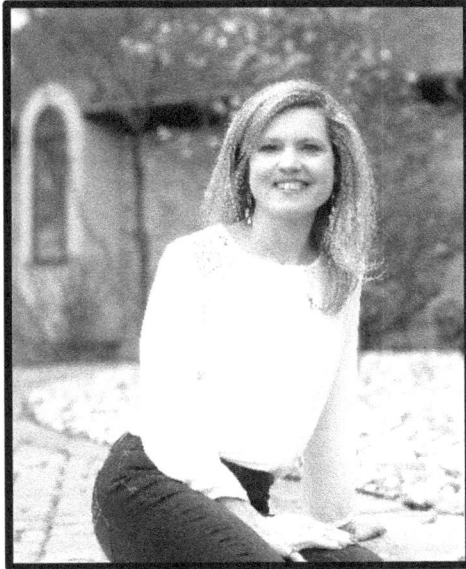

Meschelle has an active ministry helping people clearly define their priorities so they can live with balance and fulfillment. She speaks regularly for a variety of audiences including churches, women's groups, corporate and non-profit groups. You can learn more about Meschelle or contact her to speak for your group at her website:

www.meschellekolb.com

Contact Information:

mk@meschellekolb.com   574-318-8955

www.ingramcontent.com/pod-product-compliance
Lightning Source LLC
LaVergne TN
LVHW011334080426
835513LV00006B/351